The book is written by seven poets who joined their poetry together to create this. It started with Ahmad Almansoori seeking poets to create a poetry book with the aim to publish small time writers and aspiring authors.

Ahmad Almansoori

COMPENDIUM

AUSTIN MACAULEY PUBLISHERS™
LONDON • CAMBRIDGE • NEW YORK • SHARJAH

ISBN – 9789948790600 – (Paperback)
ISBN – 9789948790617 – (E-Book)

Application Number: MC-10-01-8642962
Age Classification: E

First Published 2023
AUSTIN MACAULEY PUBLISHERS FZE
Sharjah Publishing City
P.O Box [519201]
Sharjah, UAE
www.austinmacauley.ae
+971 655 95 202

List of Poets

Zayed Almazroui
Ghanem Alzaabi
Abdullah Nayssi
Ahmed Almansoori
Mira Abdullah
A.A.Y
Maitha Alblooshi

A feather plucked straight from the skies
The ink, from depths of darkest seas
And prose, to weave and hypnotize
To bring the mountains to their knees
When laid out bare to friend and foe,
One's waking dream plucked from his mind
It must go on, this dazzling show
Beside you, those with pen and ink, you'll find.
Step by step, towards dreams we stride
Our hearts beat all in swaying prose
And onwards, into the night we ride
At least, that's how the story goes.

– Zayed Almazroui

We fly toward the endless sky with a hopeful heart between our arms. The shackles of reality will always dictate our dreams. As we fall, the horrid smell of burning feathers and charred skin fill us with regrets. Yet, we still imagine a world where we soared the skies.

– Ghanem Alzaabi

Our brains are interconnected
Yet our hearts are not

You ask if I trust you
No doubt I do.
You don't lie
but you just choose
to hide away the truth.
And that I don't trust

I want to hear you speak
I want to hear you shout for god sakes.

Share with me your fears and let me know.
About me and about this and about the inferno.

What you hate, and what you don't.
We can't perfect what I don't know.

I'll tell you mine, and it's you not letting go
It's you choosing to stay with a heart that's astray

What should I do
to prove to you that it will just be us two.
Tell me what do you fear

If you don't tell me then
Why am I here.

– Abdullah Nayssi

Poetry is convoluted,
We pick and choose what we portray

All our poems would be different,
If they had all that we had to say

Still,
I'll write false poems
and absurd notions
Till my pen finds that,
that moves all emotions.

– Ahmed Almansoori

I clutch the tangled mess of strings
And poke about between the gaps
The rhyme and reason for the things
I've tried to bury in the past

The frayed edge begins to unwind
And at the string I start to pull
A cosmos, within myself I find
A child, wide-eyed and gleeful.

– Zayed Almazroui

The night exists for people with chests filled by unspoken words, with tears filled by unspoken emotions, with thoughts filled by unspoken desires. The night exists for souls with unspoken torture, for bodies with unspoken pain, for minds with unspoken terrors. The night exists for people who read these words and find comfort within the dark parts of themselves, for people who read these words and find peace with the shattered pieces of their hearts, for people who read these words and find serenity within the raging complexities of their past. The night exists for people like us to unburden ourselves, to scatter our damaged parts into the night hoping one day it gains the strength to outshine the stars and guide us through what we will soon call the beauty of life.

– Mira Abdullah

They say, "Home is not a place; it's a person."
I say that's too simplistic, too external, too fragile.

If I am a soul before I am a body,
I say Home is an illusion of safety in a world that can never
be a soul's home.

If I am a human made of stardust with a galaxy for a mind,
I say Home is a phenomenon far beyond spacetime.

If I am a subject with free will, rather than a puppet in Fate's
hands,
I say Home is where you choose to build a life; not the big,
broken house where you were born.

I say Home is where the point in which you're standing
supports the direction you're going.
Home is when your people do not anchor you into a mold to
manifest their lost dreams.
Home is when your body does not feel like a cage and your
mind an incurable disease.
Home is when your mortal humanness is not dead while it
still breathes.

Home is inside of you.
It cannot be a place because places burn,
and it cannot be a person because people leave.

– A.A.Y

Tears are rolling
Hearts are breaking
Lies are flowing
Words are controlling
Looks are deceiving
Souls are departing
And yet, here we all are
On the verge of collapsing
Thinking we are destroying
Everything that is living
When in reality
We are just surviving.

– Mira Abdullah

Your dimly lit spirit guides my path. Even when everything turned away, your light blessed me with lasting comfort. Your presence is my waking dream amidst a world that forgot how to sleep. To follow your steps is to find purpose; for you are my passion fueling my path forward.

– Ghanem Alzaabi

Arrows piercing throw the sky
Earth beckons them to land
Bodies pinned against the ground
the few survivors hand to hand.

– Ahmed Almansoori

One was of little distance yet there was distance in our
minds.
One was of great distance of land and age, yet our minds
were close as two brothers can be.
One was of no distance whatsoever, but the existence of
someone else Life taught me.

Best isn't always within beauty.

Life taught me, best isn't always within my age.
Life taught me, best isn't always within no one.
Life taught me, best isn't always within my reach.

– Abdullah Nayssi

In my mind,
there's a strange connection between love and mirrors.

I look at a mirror, I do not find love.
Then I look at the one I love, and I find a mirror –
I feel mirrored.

And it is here, through unconditionally loving another,
that I find my impossible conditions for loving myself
crumbling before my eyes.

I look at the same mirror again,
I remember that I forgot that I am only human,
And relief washes over me as I finally find a lovable woman.

– A.A.Y

Never stood in front of a mirror

Frightened she was, as the flashes were near her

Frightened she was, as the reflections were near her

Deep thoughts and comprehension, reflections and mirrors
did not frighten her

She fell in love with what she saw, she fell in love with
herself and her mirrors.

– Maitha Alblooshi

How glamorous is an evening with nothing but silence.
I'd dare call it a holy night, for it inspires my soul in many
levels.
The ticking of the clock signals the end of a peaceful day. I
only pray that tonight is the longest night to ever come.

– Ghanem Alzaabi

Love in pure form
High winds on thunderstorms
Wave on wave they clash
But never do they crash.

– Ahmed Almansoori

As the last petal falls off the rose, all that we are left with are the thorns of a bitter-sweet memory. As the last ray of sunshine hits the ocean, all that we are left with are the feelings of an empty promise. As the last drop of rain hits the pavement, all that we are left with are the disillusions of a fantasy. As the last grain of sand fills up the beach, all that we are left with are the drowning sorrows of nostalgia. As the lifespan of a butterfly comes to an end, all that we are left with is an overwhelming sense of hopelessness. As the universe finally lets go of the gravity of life, all that we are left with is a destructive dark hole waiting to be filled. As the touch of a loved one seeps through my fingers, all that I am left with is the yearning of more. As the base of my dress is swept away as I dance, all that I am left with is a trail of what was once beautiful. As the trace of his kiss stains my right cheek, all that I am left with is the desire of a lost thing. As the softness of the sheets entangle with my legs, all that I am left with is darkness to soothe my pain. As the lotion spreads across my body, all that I am left with is an intense feeling of abandonment. As the door finally shuts close against the solidity of my back, all I am left with is a shattered shell devoid of any soul.

— Mira Abdullah

You remind me of the morning sky…
The way you blush as you undress like pink clouds that
appear after the dark starry night has disappeared…
Show me more of you…
I want to know if you can remind me of the evening sky as
well…
If you can show me how to feel the colors of red, orange,
yellow, purple, pink, and
blue deep within the essence of my soul…
You remind me of honey being drizzled on pancakes…
The way your smile fills every inch of me like the perfect
ratio of sweetness and
warmth after having your first bite of dessert…
Show me more of you…
I want to know if you can remind me of a home-cooked
meal…
If you can show me how to feel the burst of flavors with
every inhale as it settles in
the pit of my stomach with satisfaction…
You remind me of flowers in the spring…
The way you bloom unexpectedly like lavender on a breezy
afternoon…
show me more of you…

– Mira Abdullah

In Search of Identity Through Solitude
My need for solitude is insatiable.
I lock my doors and dive deep into myself,
looking for something without even knowing what it is.
Sometimes answers appear in the ceiling of my room;
sometimes I find myself locked in for weeks.

Sliding into a dark labyrinth
with a flashlight running low on battery,
I strive to grasp a hint,
a little clue as to who I am and why I'm here.
Trace back to the past,
untangle this mystery of my mind.
Leap towards the future,
make a promise to the unknown:

I'll find my way through the maze;
I'll come to you knowing more than I know now;
I'll refine my inner world in this timeless solitude
To welcome you right here into my present at last.

I surrender to the possibilities:
Perhaps being me is a journey of continuous transformation;
perhaps I am here on a higher quest for self-actualization;

perhaps there is no one answer for all my questions;
perhaps the real answer is to make peace with no answer.

– A.A.Y

27

Bring the ruined through the door
The beastly cries, the starlit floor
The midnight, burning candles tall
The maidens, dancing through the halls
A name, once screamed, twice whispered slow
A priest, to call the final blow
And when the morning hurries past,
We'll all be woken once at last.

– Zayed Almazroui

Hollow ears
To my echoes
Caverns, Caverns
Do you hear
Or is my voice
never near.

– Ahmed Almansoori

I fall in love with my lover's name
as though he's the Adam of this Earth
the first man, the only man
my two eyes, the oxygen to my lungs

I hope and pray and plead
please God
let this be the last name that feels like a song
let this be the name with whom I build my life

a name that contains all the world's languages
a name that breathes life into my poems

a name that cures my speechlessness
a name that answers to my silences

a name that contains three letters of mine
leaving the fourth all to me
for he and I, we are whole before we are one

a name after which mine always comes
I call it, and it calls mine
I call it again, like a child uttering her only word
awaiting the same response as though it's the first time
oh God
seal my fate

forbid me from uttering another
and feeling the slightest flutter
my lips are already heavy
his is the only name that feels light to me
it rolls through my lips like a lullaby
grounds me to Earth, to life, to Him
sends me flying up to Heaven, to me, to us

– A.A.Y

I want to know if you can remind me of the unseen roots of
nature…
If you can show me how to feel the strength and steadiness
of my body as I lay safely
in your arms…
Show me more of you…
I cannot seem to get enough…
Show me more of you…
The thought of you consumes me with joy…
Show me more of you…
I promise I'll take nothing but my memories…
Show me more of you…
Maybe one day I'll show you a part of me but until then…
Show me more of you.

– Mira Abdullah

Is my life an enigma?

A paradox, perhaps?

My mind is full of flowing thoughts

unanswered questions

Lost in the mines of my consciousness

Oh dear, let's hold on a bit tighter to our stars

We shall see if those complex thoughts land on Pluto or
Mars.

– Maitha Alblooshi

A mistake I made of looking ahead
Maybe I looked too far I've been misled
You were the first person I laid eyes on
And the first to have known
A flair lit up as I glanced upon you
Not knowing what to do
I said she is special, unique from them
A bit shy, but crazy in her own way
Unknowingly beautiful, stunning I should say
She's someone I'd like to know
Late but I'll try a simple hello.

– Abdullah Nayssi

My obliviousness caused enormous damage

I never wanted to create this emotional baggage

Sorry is a tiny word, it might not fix the breakage

Give me a chance and let me divulge;

You're important to me and I pledge

To love you forever and put an end to the damage.

– Maitha Alblooshi

Oh morning wind, whose soft caress
Passed gently, warm and bold
What secrets do you carry?
Whose whispers do you hold?
Which lover blew a midnight kiss
And through you, gave it flight?
How kind of you to guarantee
It's safety through the night.

– Zayed Almazroui

I spread my pages to be read
But they are just scorned instead
I'm not an open book
My pages are not widespread
It would not hurt this much if they were
They only opened once and that was to her.

– Ahmed Almansoori

Moon dust fill my lungs
Star light pierce my eyes
Choking on words that will cause your demise

A love with the heat of a thousand suns
Now crushing me with what weighs a ton

With a desires only you could tame
Silence from you is all that came

A love perhaps that will never be
A love between myself and thee.

– Zayed Almazroui

So when you tell me you love me… paint me a picture… Paint me a picture of how many times you can say it without saying it… I do not think it would be possible if the roles were reversed… If I were to tell you that I love you… I would stutter through every syllable making sure the words stretch long enough for me to enunciate every emotion, every thought, every word, every action into the phrase… If I were to tell you that I love you… I would collect every teardrop, every heartbeat, every pupil dilation, every shaky breath and give it to you so you can feel the lightness of those words against the heaviness of my actions… If I were to tell you that I love you… you wouldn't be able to handle it because the love I have for you could stabilize earthquakes, it could destroy hurricanes, it could take out tsunamis, it could extinguish wildfires… If I were to tell you that I love you… you wouldn't accept it because you can only accept the love you think you deserve and while you may need my love desperately, you do not think you deserve it so you reject it… that is okay, I guess we're not so different after all… I guess that's why our love works together so well… I guess that is why we never leave because it has become too familiar… rejecting the love we offer to each other while simultaneously giving each other the same love we reject.

– Mira Abdullah

I enjoyed your laugh
as it humored me for more.

I enjoyed your voice
as it told me for more
I enjoyed your eyes
as they made me look for more
I enjoyed your words
as they sentenced me for more

but when I got to your smile
it gave me a reason to want more

I enjoyed everything
until I realized it was all for nothing.
I enjoyed wanting more
but I never got anything, just more of more.

– Abdullah Nayssi

Love comes and goes,
heals and breaks,
comes and goes again,
heals and breaks again.

That's the cycle,
and only true love can endure.

But sometimes,
even the most real of all love
must give in to the harshness of reality.

Because when love feels like Heaven on Earth,
maybe it's a sign that it belongs to the afterlife.

– A.A.Y

I'd like to be a London poet
In 1954

I'd be a baker
Slapping dough in the
Morning

And in the night, with letters
Mourning.

– Ahmad Almansoori

I cannot cut into you anymore
You have become too precious
You have become important
So now all I can do is fantasize
About the way the blood drips from your body
About the way the cool blade feels against your warm skin
About the way the hot tears cause trails of regret on your
face
It is getting harder to merely fantasize anymore
So I pick up the blade once more
I mean… What's another tiny cut in a museum of scars?

– Mira Abdullah

Wings made of paper
And spine filled with ink
Stomach that hungers
But only for thought

Leave me days for contemplation
To stretch every muscle, fiber and strand in pursuit of
imagination
And let me run
But not on earth
Let me run like the sky's a carpet
Laid on marble flooring
Afterwards, Ill choose no hearth
No place to take this feeling while I have it

Unless it's a dream that the sun calls away as it calls the
morning.

– Ahmed Almansoori

From all of these I've learnt so much
With so much left to learn.
While some laid brick and made a home,
Some stay as only memories
With so many bridges burned

It's time to give my warmest thanks
And send them on their way
For no one knows what 'morrow brings
And in the past, the past remains
We're left with nothing but today.

– Zayed Almazroui

I wish when we are together,
We are truly so
I don't bring my world with me,
I put it aside

Cause no world compares to you by my side
It's where all my sorrows are put to rest
And where all my thoughts decide to hide

It's truly where am my best

With an avalanche to you I'd ride
Amidst a storm that never rests.

– Ahmed Almansoori

According to these earthlings, the moon is merely a rock and the sun a bright star. They do not know any better because they are not ready for the truth, for the pain, for the love, for the journey, for the intimacy, for the heartbreak, for the romance, for the epic union between the moon and the sun. They do not know about the reasons the moon circles the planet daily and the reasons why the sun dims its light at certain hours of the day. They do not know about the secret dates and the intense fleeting moments of agony during every sunrise and every sunset. They do not know about the days when the sun sets so beautifully that even the moon cannot resist watching it go.

They do not know about the mornings when the moon has to leave so the sun rises early as an attempt to bid it farewell until their next encounter. They do not know about the nights when the sun offers its light to the moon so it doesn't get lost in the dark. They do not know that it is the only way the sun can guarantee its lover will find its way back to it. They do not know about the moon's sorrow or the sun's passion.

They do not know about the beauty of the moon's journey of healing. They do not know about the ways the sun chooses to love itself as it continues to burn magnificently regardless of the moon's presence. They do not know about this beautiful and torturous everlasting desire between them but then again, how can they when they haven't begun to understand the beauty and desire within themselves yet?

– Mira Abdullah

Tinker, thinker. Toil and trouble.
Through the endless, awful rubble.
Maybe, someday, it shall pass;
Maybe you'll be left to struggle

Past the strife and past the sorrow,
Past the longings for tomorrow.
Holding steadfast, built to last
Through storm that leave you bare and hollow
(For last, the storms, your soul would swallow).

– Zayed Almazroui

I'm an empty shell of what I once was. Did I grow, so
magically so out of a cocoon?
Or did I fall into a cesspit with no hope in sight? I find
myself pondering such
questions at night. I'm oblivious of whether this is an omen
of good or ill
fate, but I'll keep marching forward.

– Ghanem Alzaabi

I just realized that a building floor is sometimes called a story or stories. This means that every single room in the floor has a story of its own, people living their own lives, each individual with a thousand stories to tell.

– Ghanem Alzaabi

I owe the pleasures of today
To those who came before;
The empty cup that taught me pain,
Or trust taught by a broken clock.
I could not ask for more.

A book, shut tight, once spoke to me
And, in the softest tone,
Said, "Let go of your comforts, there is
More to life than meets the eye,
Much more than what you own."

Daffodils, all in a bunch,
Came to me in a dream.
Presented me my inner child
And spoke of knight, and war, and love
From places yet unseen.

– Zayed Almazroui

Cathartic conclusions break mental illusions
The kind that just lingers and holds
As trapped as we are in our inner confusions
There's hope that we'd break through the mold
For longing and wanting and wishing and hoping
May very much keep us alive
It's always in seeing what lies behind feeling
That gives us our will to survive.

– Zayed Almazroui

Epilogue

To all the poets and the dreamers
The first stone is laid
The first strokes on it portrayed
A slate is laying on it
Waiting for your name to be engraved

– Ahmed Almansoori

www.ingramcontent.com/pod-product-compliance
Lightning Source LLC
Chambersburg PA
CBHW070607160726
48003CB00005B/2151